# Barn Quilt

## Poems

by Maria Glymph

A Modern Odyssey Book

ISBN: 979-8-9900395-1-3

www.modernodysseybooks.com

For Tom
my beloved

For Kristin

In homage to Gary

# Author's Note

Each poem in this collection stands alone. And yet, collectively these poems are a narrative — one of friendship, grief, loss, and wonder. For a few weeks last year, my husband and I spent time with dear friends facing a life-threatening illness. The setting was the North Carolina farmland, teaming with breath and movement and color. All the while, the gloom of a deteriorating situation loomed. Our friends, bound together for over forty years, were coming to terms with a parting. We also understood that it was the occasion for goodbyes. The moments together were cherished, and the gifts abundant. Barn Quilt is that experience.

M.G.

# Contents

# On Sydnor Farm

In the rising morning light
before the sun has decided to stand upright,
the shadows sleep and the meadows stir.

The pink hibiscus open their throats,
lapping up the drops from the daybreak watering,
bees dive deep to fish out nectar.

He is here

Inside the hen house, low voices
from talk radio crackle stories and
dispatch the chickens into the yard.

The gourds inch slowly on their knees,
arms grabbing and groping,
leaves like outstretched palms.

He is here

The corrugated shed shelters the unemployed truck,
and a gathering of equipment stands in line out front
waiting turns, hoping for some work.

The barn positioned on a grass runway,
ready to take flight with its parallel porches
outstretched wings.

He is here

Monarchs and swallowtails prance
across the lantana, darting and flitting
between trees and shrubs.

The greenhouse set firm like a temple.
Planter boxes worship the sun,
an overflowing treasure of nightshade jewels.

He is here

A charm of hummingbirds performs
a circle dance, intoxicated by
the candied water and the fresh morning air.

A pine tree stands alone in a puddle of dried needles,
a gnomon, loitering, pointing toward the bird feeder.
Zinnias and gladiolus sway to the rhythm of the day.

He is here

The front pastures sit idle, waiting for
the cows and the sheep to crest the horizon
and bring their curiosity and their hunger.

A family of raccoons crosses the gravel drive
which cuts a stream to the road
beyond this Eden.

# Love Song

Huddled together they climb
nourished by the flame of the ancient star,
Adam's ale and her tears.

Arranged in the flower box,
upright like colored pencils –
fuchsia, tangerine, ivory, salmon, gold.
The season of singing, started.

She hovers over him low,
tucking his blanket secure,
thumping his pillows fluffy,
changing his bandages clean,
whispering her affection deep.

They produce flowers until the first frost.
For everything there is a season.

She scatters the seeds,
running a hand rake through the soil.

From darkness they will grow.

Soon she will harvest the bounty of color,
fill a vase with tears and arrange her grief.

Then, she will dance.

# Hen House

Under the shade of the live oak
they scratch and peck
sprint and cluck
gossip and dream

If only, the weight of a rooster
If only, a touching kiss

# In the Hollow of His Hand

He steps down from the truck's running board
as if descending from a pedestal,
cradling two beers in the hollow of his Rodin hands.

Face and neck are red from the open air,
blond eyebrows awnings over alpine eyes.
His volume moves freely in Round House
rolled to the calf – a bull with socked feet.

He visits daily, checking cows, bush hogging, hauling trash.
They jaw about the Rocky Mount tornado, raising sheep,
the billion-dollar lottery, and calves coming early.
Both shapeshift between a menagerie of animals –
lion, lamb, tiger, lark, monkey, mule.

As the afternoon runs toward the horizon, he rises to leave.
Standing behind the recliner, he bends to whisper
cupping the nodding head in the hollow of his hands.

# Barn Quilt

patchwork of pastures
threaded by fences
seams of community

beacons signaling
across low hills and
creek bottoms

commemorations
as ornamental patterns
adorn barns

# Submerged

I wonder what it's like for her, as she escapes from the hospital, driving out of the parking garage, following the track of highway, and entering the protection of her home. Does she, even now, hear the loudspeaker and the incessant beeps announcing the end of an IV or the change of vitals. Are the lights soft and yellow or does her vision have a veneer of bright white sterility? It seems unoriginal to wonder if she hugs her daughter tight and insist that she eat all her broccoli before going outside to catch fireflies. I imagine that she runs her fingers through her husband's wavy hair as she closes her eyes and thinks of the patients she has tended to today, praying, silently, that she never sits across from someone like herself. How many times will she utter a meaningless *Sorry*? How many times will she barely suppress a banshee scream as she faces a man who has no options. His wife sitting alongside, gripping his hand, pools of pain flooding her eyes and threatening to submerge the room? Of what can she be proud? Where is the line between success and failure? Between hope and whatever is the opposite?

# Dilapidated Barns

rustic roads are littered
kneeling barns and emaciated sheds
remnants of their former selves
grey hair, hollow eyes, empty souls
unkempt

shunned
they squat in fields of tall fescue
crouch amid oak trees
sit among wildflowers

they tell their stories to the wind
and any passing animal that has ears to hear

## 25 Miles

*for Tracy*

The town inhabited us. We knew
its rooms, its hidden passageways,
its arcades,

the dual meaning of *Keep Out*,
the feigned prohibition of the speakeasy,
the contents of the bank.

To know a place is to newly define distance,
fingerprints fade, personal graffiti
conceals, remembrances erode.

When you draw a circle, someone is on the outside,
peering over the circumference.
And then a stranger comes to town.

My father was skeptical.
She wasn't from around here.

# Jeopardy

After the six o'clock news on Channel 11
we join the other contestants on Jeopardy

They: playing to win, thousands of dollars,
a Cancun vacation, shopping in New York

We: playing not to lose, his life, his contest
with cancer, the trial with treatment

Every night, currency is played for profit
and for loss, to obtain wealth either way

We leave nothing unspent, and as our pockets
empty our shoes weigh down our steps

What wouldn't we give to be in their place
What wouldn't they give to not be in ours

Time: a moment of distraction
Money: the illusion of wealth

# Labyrinth Walk

Hear me

I beseech you,
their unwavering love is threatened
by the Minotaur meandering the hospital halls
– a labyrinth of illness and affliction,
malady mingled with faltering hope

I fear the beast

Hear me

## Buoyancy

In the time he's been buoyant
he has left the earth and matter
behind.

Feeling like Neil Armstrong.
Floating weightless in a salty pool,
a lake of tears in the black of space.

Not the first to set foot
on craters of grief, these fine grains
of emotion are a new exploration.

The balls of his feet touch bottom
as he bounces. Heaviness in his heart.
Gravity pulls from poolside.

He has no flag to plant,
no pronouncement to make,
no mission to accomplish.

Instead, he floats
and when it's time,
he will leave his footprints
behind.

## Radar

the anxious alarm
radar by default
robbing him
at intervals
predetermined times
nourishment, medication
echo

life confiscated by time
held without freedom
robbing him
by reminding him
of time
unspent

Time leaves its mark
in the moment
and in remembrance –

I choose my memories
having changed the default
on all my devices

# Miraculous Ordinary

Like a barmaid, she dispenses the drink of the earth,
taking exhausted buds and yellowed leaves as tips

Like a chef, she fills dispensers and feeds bird and beasts,
nourishing the multitudes

Like an accountant, she checks inventory,
drafting the list of dog treats, lard, bird seed, and milk

Like a masseuse, she caresses the soft manes of the animals,
handing out warmth with her touch

Like a farmhand, she breaks for lunch to sit
under the outstretch arms of the elm, squinting the afternoon

With the blanket of darkness and a downy pillow, she will curl up
and welcome fatigue to narrate her dreams

# Regret

Tell me if you have regrets

Tell me if your luggage is lighter

Tell me if you have coins in your pockets

Tell me if you left words unsaid to your parents

Tell me if today's story is a rough draft

Tell me if your glasses of memory need cleaning

Tell me if you've withheld forgiveness

Tell me if some dreams have mermaids

Tell me if you enter and leave a room differently

Tell me if you have amends left to make

Tell me if there are words that leave you hungry

Tell me if you'd like to laugh more

Tell me if you would choose a different path

Tell me if you think it would have brought you here

# In the Weeping

He lays wait
in the shadow
of the weeping cherry
stalking
growing impatient

He comes to collect
payment
for living
inevitable is fate
the rotating spool

He strikes
through the door
grabbing the scissors
snipping
the dogs yawn in place

He knows
destiny is written
before the time
of mythology

# Cardinal

The red cardinal pecks
at his doppelganger
like a machine gun.

Peering at his reflection
with the intensity of Narcissus.

Wearing his peaked hat
and bright feathers
as battle garments.

Enduring daily invasions
from formidable opponents.

Defending his love
for her, forever loyal.

Knowing the spoils of war.
She will never famine.

## Final Morning

In three days you'll be dead.

But today, you walk us to the car,
too healthy for hospice.

This goodbye comes with a full stop,
and all our stories become past tense.

I've never fully grasped how the telephone works.
Sound waves. Electrical energy. Vibrations.

It does though, and similarly I believe by faith
we'll be together again, somewhere
on that side, wherever that is, however we travel.

# Tribute to G

You did not live myth
So many stories written
Hero with your face

## Barn of Spirits

*for Gary*

He is careful not to scrape the peaks of his knuckles
turning the knob that sits too close to the jamb.
He knees the door, and with his left hand
steadies the sign that declares the spirits within.

As always, he is too late for the clang of the bell
and just in time for the rush of air that receives him
like an old friend, embracing him with a dance of dirt and dust.

Inside, a storm of hooves and a whirlwind of sand and silt and soil
twirling and circling in a swirl of speed: past winners.

They race around the braided rug, and straight away
Seattle Slew is out front, Flying Ebony second, Old Rosebud drafting
behind by a length, Foolish Pleasure, Always Dreaming, Dark Star
on the outside, fast as wildfire, they fly.

The stakes: brown liquor. Bulleit, Blanton's, Basil Hayden,
Elijah Craig, Kentucky Owl, Maker's Mark,
Sazerac, Knob Creek, and of course, Woodford Reserve.

Around the turn, Street Sense makes a move to the inside,
Black Gold charges from behind and the kaleidoscope of jerseys
bobs up and down. Strike for strike, stride for stride.

It's the top of the stretch, Always Dreaming has taken the lead.
The pace is hot, the sound is a blizzard, and the winner is...

The horse determines the label as he blows the dust off the tumbler.
He exits through the back door. The birds scatter like seeds.
The rocker begins its slow sonorous arrangement,
and the first sip stings in the middle of his chest.
He nods to the cows across the pond.

# Acknowledgments

Enormous thanks to Doug, Shannon, Tracy, and Josh for their kindness, warmth, and welcome during our time in North Carolina. And, for the inspiration they provided — it is found in these pages.

Huge thank you to Claire, Susan, Tom, and Cindy for their very thoughtful reading, suggestions and support.

Deep gratitude to Kristin for friendship, trust, and example.

And to Tom, for everything, always.

# About the Author

Maria Glymph is a writer and the publisher of
Modern Odyssey Books.
This is her first volume of poetry.